How To Master Digital Detox

Build Good Habits, Improve Focus, Develop Personal
Management Skills and Achieve Long Term Success
in Life.

PRADIP DAS

are declared or implied. Readers acknowledge that the author is not engaging in the rendering of legal, financial, medical or professional advice. The content within this book has been derived from various sources. Please consult a licensed professional before attempting any techniques outlined in this book.

By reading this document, the reader agrees that under no circumstances is the author responsible for any losses, direct or indirect, which are incurred as a result of the use of information contained within this document, including, but not limited to, — errors, omissions, or inaccuracies.

*Please scan for the other books of the **"Life Mastery"** Series.*

Table of Contents

About The Book

In a world dominated by digital devices and constant connectivity, finding moments of peace and balance is like a daunting task. *"How To Master Digital Detox"* offers a refreshing perspective on reclaiming control of our digital lives and rediscovering the joys of being present in the moment.

This book is not about exclusion technology entirely; rather, it's a guide to striking a healthy balance between our digital world and the real world. Through practical tips and insightful advice, it empowers readers to like a journey of self-discovery and mindfulness.

Whether you are feeling overwhelmed by the constant noise of notifications, struggling to disconnect from social media, or simply craving a break from the digital noise, this book offers a roadmap to freedom. From setting clear boundaries to cultivating mindfulness, each chapter is filled with actionable steps to help you detoxify your digital habits and embrace a more fulfilling, offline existence.

More than just a guidebook, *"How To Master Digital Detox"* is a reminder that true happiness and fulfillment lie not in the endless scroll of a screen, but in the richness of real-life experiences, meaningful connections, and moments of quiet reflection.

Whether you are ready to accept a full-blown digital detox or simply looking for ways to strike a healthier balance, this book will be your trusted companion on the journey towards reclaiming your time, your attention, and ultimately, your life.

Introduction

In a quiet neighborhood with pretty gardens and chirping birds, lived the Thompson family. They were always happy and close-knit, with children laughing, the smell of homemade cookies, and lots of love.

But when technology started taking over their lives, things changed. The kids spent more time on screens, and the family started drifting apart. Dinners became quiet because everyone was busy on their phones or tablets. The warmth of family time was replaced by the glow of screens, making everyone feel lonely. Weekends used to be fun with family outings, but now the kids preferred staying inside with their gadgets. This made the parents sad, missing the days when they would all laugh and have fun together.

As the family argued more about screen time, they realized that they were growing apart. They felt distant and frustrated with each other. But they also realized that real happiness comes from spending time together, not from screens. With tears in their eyes, the Thompson family decided to make a change. They set limits on screen time and started spending more time together. Slowly, they found joy in each other's company again.

Their story shows that love and resilience can overcome any challenge. Even when things seem dark, there's always hope for a brighter future. As the Thompsons put away their screens and focused on each other, they rediscovered the simple joys of being a family.

The Digital Age Dilemma

Same way, I found myself entangled in a story all too familiar to many across the globe. My job demanded that I stay connected every hour of every day, tying me to my phone like a prisoner to their cell.

In this digital realm, WhatsApp became my battleground. Messages poured in relentlessly, each one clamoring for my attention. From work updates to immediate action, my phone buzzed non-stop, making it nearly impossible to catch a break. And because my job required me to be online all the time, escaping the digital world seemed like an impossible feat.

Now, don't get me wrong, I managed to steer clear of the temptations of social media giants like Facebook and Instagram. But even without them, the sheer volume of messages flooding my WhatsApp inbox was enough to overwhelm me. And as much as I wanted to take a break from the digital madness, finding a way to disconnect felt like trying to break free from a powerful spell.

But here's where things get tricky. While I was caught up in the digital whirlwind, my family life began to suffer. My loved ones felt the impact of my constant digital tethering, and it created tension in our home. Despite recognizing the need for a break, I felt stuck in a cycle of digital dependence, unable to find a way out.

So there I was, a character in a digital tale, longing for a break from the chaos but unsure how to escape. And as the digital world continued to spin around me, I couldn't help but wonder: would I ever find my way back to a simpler, more connected life?

But it is not me only, in today's world, it seems everyone is glued to their screens with or without compulsion. Whether it's smartphones, tablets, or laptops, digital devices have become an integral part of our daily lives. We use them to stay connected with friends and family, to work, to shop, and to entertain ourselves. But while technology has undoubtedly made our lives more convenient in many ways, it has also brought about a host of challenges and dilemmas.

One of the biggest dilemmas of the digital age is the constant struggle to find a balance between our online and offline lives. On one hand, technology allows us to stay connected with people from all over the world, to access a wealth of information at our fingertips, and to streamline many aspects of our daily routines. But on the other hand, it can also lead to feelings of isolation, distraction, and even addiction.

For many people, the lines between work and personal life have become increasingly blurred in the digital age. With the rise of remote work and the prevalence of smartphones, it's all too easy to find ourselves checking emails or responding to work-related messages long after we've left the office. This constant connectivity can take a toll on our mental health, leading to increased stress, anxiety, and burnout.

Another dilemma of the digital age is the impact of technology on our relationships. While digital devices allow us to stay connected with friends and family members across the globe, they can also create barriers to meaningful communication. How often have we seen couples out to dinner together, each staring at their phones instead of engaging with one another? Or parents spending more time scrolling through social media than playing with their children? These are just a few examples of how technology can erode the quality of our relationships and lead to feelings of disconnection and loneliness.

Then there's the issue of information overload. In today's digital age, we have access to more information than ever before, but sorting through it all can be overwhelming. We're bombarded with news, social media updates, emails, and notifications on a constant basis, making it difficult to separate fact from fiction and to focus on what truly matters. This constant barrage of information can leave us feeling mentally exhausted and unable to concentrate on the tasks at hand.

But perhaps the biggest dilemma of the digital age is the impact of technology on our mental health and well-being. Studies have shown that excessive screen time can lead to a host of negative outcomes, including poor sleep quality, decreased physical activity, and increased risk of depression and anxiety. And yet, many of us find ourselves unable to break free from the pull of our digital devices, even when we know they're having a detrimental effect on our health.

So, what can we do to navigate the digital age dilemma? The first step is to become more mindful of our technology use and its impact on our lives. This means setting boundaries around screen time, taking regular breaks from digital devices, and prioritizing face-to-face interactions with loved ones. It also means being more selective about the information we consume and learning to disconnect from technology when it's not serving us in a positive way.

Ultimately, finding a healthy balance in the digital age requires conscious effort and intentionality. By taking steps to prioritize our mental health, nurture our relationships, and cultivate mindfulness in our technology use, we can navigate the challenges of the digital age with greater ease and grace. And in doing so, we can reclaim control over our lives and rediscover the joy and fulfillment that comes from living in the present moment.

Understanding Digital Dependency

Now, it is hard to imagine life without digital devices like smartphones, computers, and tablets. These gadgets have become an integral part of our daily lives, helping us stay connected, informed, and entertained. However, as we rely more and more on technology, it's important to understand the concept of digital dependency and its impact on our well-being.

Digital dependency refers to the psychological and emotional reliance on digital devices and the internet. It's the feeling of being unable to function properly without constant access to technology. Just like any other dependency, such as addiction to drugs or alcohol, digital dependency can have serious consequences for our mental and physical health if left unchecked. One of the main reasons people become digitally dependent is the instant gratification that technology provides. With just a few taps on a screen, we can access a world of information, entertainment, and social interaction. This instant gratification can be addictive, leading us to spend more and more time on our devices in search of that next dopamine hit.

Another factor that contributes to digital dependency is the fear of missing out, or FOMO.

Social media platforms like Facebook, Instagram, and Twitter constantly bombard us with updates and notifications, making us feel like we need to constantly check our feeds to stay in the loop. This fear of missing out can drive us to spend hours scrolling through our timelines, even when we have more important things to do.

Digital dependency can also stem from a need for validation and approval from others. Social media platforms have made it easier than ever to seek validation from our peers through likes, comments, and shares. This constant need for validation can lead to an unhealthy obsession with our online persona, causing us to prioritize digital interactions over real-life relationships.

The consequences of digital dependency can be far-reaching and profound. Excessive screen time has been linked to a variety of physical health issues, including eye strain, headaches, and sleep disturbances. Mentally, digital dependency can contribute to anxiety, depression, and feelings of isolation and loneliness. It can also negatively impact our relationships with friends, family, and coworkers, as we become increasingly absorbed in our digital lives at the expense of real-life connections.

So, how can we break free from digital dependency and regain control of our lives? The first step is awareness—recognizing the signs of digital dependency and acknowledging the negative impact it's having on our well-being. Once we've identified the problem, we can take proactive steps to reduce our reliance on technology and establish healthier habits.

One effective strategy for reducing digital dependency is setting boundaries and limits around our device usage. This could involve setting designated "screen-free" times or zones in our homes, such as during meals or before bedtime. We can also try scheduling regular breaks from our devices throughout the day to give our minds and bodies a chance to recharge.

Another important step is cultivating mindfulness and presence in our daily lives. Instead of mindlessly scrolling through our social media feeds or constantly checking our emails, we can try to be more intentional about how we use our digital devices. This could involve practicing mindfulness techniques, such as deep breathing or meditation, to help us stay grounded and present in the moment.

Building strong real-life connections is also crucial for overcoming digital dependency. Instead of relying solely on digital communication to stay in touch with friends and family, we can make an effort to spend more time together in person. Whether it's going for a walk, having a coffee date, or simply enjoying a conversation without distractions, nurturing our real-life relationships can help reduce our dependence on technology.

Finally, it's important to remember that breaking free from digital dependency is a journey, not a destination. It may take time and effort to establish new habits and routines, but the rewards—greater peace of mind, improved relationships, and a deeper connection to the world around us—are well worth the effort.

Digital dependency is a widespread issue in today's society, with far-reaching consequences for our mental and physical health. By understanding the root causes of digital dependency and taking proactive steps to address them, we can reclaim control of our lives and cultivate a healthier relationship with technology.

Please check the Book Series of
"The Art of Living"

Understanding Digital Detox

Digital detox refers to taking a break from technology and disconnecting from digital devices for a period of time. It's a way to step back from the constant distractions of emails, social media, and notifications, and to reconnect with ourselves and the world around us. And in today's fast-paced, hyper-connected society, it's more important than ever.

One of the main reasons why digital detox is necessary is the impact that constant digital stimulation can have on our mental health. Studies have shown that excessive screen time can lead to feelings of anxiety, stress, and depression. The constant barrage of information and notifications can overwhelm our brains and leave us feeling drained and exhausted. Taking a break from technology allows our minds to rest and recharge, reducing feelings of stress and improving overall mental well-being.

Another reason why digital detox is important is the effect that it can have on our relationships. In today's digital age, it's all too easy to get caught up in our screens and neglect the people around us. Whether it's constantly checking our phones during dinner with family or spending more time scrolling through social media than engaging in meaningful conversations with friends, technology can create barriers between us and the people we care about. By taking a break from technology, we can reconnect with our loved ones and strengthen our relationships, fostering deeper connections and more meaningful interactions.

Digital detox also offers physical benefits. Spending too much time sitting in front of screens can lead to a sedentary lifestyle, which in turn can contribute to health problems such as obesity, diabetes, and heart disease. Taking a break from technology encourages us to get up and move, whether it's going for a walk outside, playing sports, or engaging in other physical activities. This not only improves our physical health but also boosts our mood and energy levels.

In addition to the mental, emotional, and physical benefits, digital detox can also enhance our productivity and creativity. Constant digital stimulation can hinder our ability to focus and concentrate, making it difficult to get things done. By taking a break from technology, we can clear our minds and sharpen our focus, allowing us to be more productive and creative in our work and personal lives.

Despite the many benefits of digital detox, many people find it difficult to disconnect from technology. We live in a society that values constant connectivity and instant gratification, making it challenging to break free from the digital cycle. However, with a little effort and determination, it is possible to incorporate digital detox into our lives and reap the rewards.

There are many ways to practice digital detox, from taking short breaks throughout the day to unplugging completely for a weekend or longer. Whatever approach you choose, the important thing is to prioritize your well-being and make time to disconnect from technology regularly. By doing so, you can enjoy the many benefits of digital detox and reclaim control over your digital life.

Digital detox is about taking a step back from technology and giving ourselves the opportunity to reset and recharge. It's like taking a vacation for our minds, allowing us to break free from the cycle of constant stimulation and give our brains a chance to rest.

But what exactly does digital detox entail? It can be as simple as setting aside designated times each day to disconnect from our devices, whether it's during meals, before bed, or during family time. It can also involve more extended breaks, such as weekends or even full-blown vacations, where we leave our devices behind entirely and immerse ourselves in the present moment.

The benefits of digital detox are numerous. For starters, it can help reduce stress and anxiety by giving us a break from the constant barrage of information and demands for our attention. It can also improve our sleep quality, as the blue light emitted by screens can disrupt our natural sleep patterns and leave us feeling groggy and unrested.

Digital detox can also improve our relationships with others. When we're constantly glued to our screens, we miss out on valuable opportunities to connect with the people around us. By taking a break from our devices, we can foster deeper connections with friends and family, and truly be present in the moments we share with them.

Moreover, digital detox can increase our productivity and creativity. When we're not constantly distracted by notifications and social media, we have more time and mental space to focus on the tasks at hand and tap into our creative potential.

Of course, digital detox isn't always easy. In a world where technology is so deeply ingrained in our daily lives, it can be challenging to break free from its grip. But by taking small steps and gradually incorporating digital detox into our routines, we can reap the benefits and find greater balance and happiness in our lives.

What is Digital Detox?

Digital detox is essentially taking a break from all things digital—think social media, email, texting, streaming services, and anything else that keeps you glued to a screen. It's about disconnecting from the digital world for a set period of time to give yourself a much-needed breather and reconnect with the real world.

Now, you might be wondering, why on earth would anyone want to do that? Well, the truth is, while technology has undoubtedly made our lives easier and more convenient in many ways, it has also brought with it a host of negative effects, both on our physical and mental well-being.

For starters, spending too much time on screens can wreak havoc on our sleep patterns. The blue light emitted by devices messes with our circadian rhythms, making it harder to fall asleep at night and leading to poor-quality sleep overall.

And we all know how important sleep is for our overall health and functioning!

But it's not just our sleep that suffers. Excessive screen time has also been linked to a range of other health issues, from eye strain and headaches to neck and back pain. Not to mention the impact it can have on our posture and physical fitness if we're spending hours hunched over our devices.

Then there's the mental toll. Constantly checking our phones and scrolling through social media feeds can leave us feeling anxious, stressed, and even depressed. It's easy to fall into the trap of comparing ourselves to others online, which can take a serious toll on our self-esteem and mental health.

But perhaps the biggest problem with our digital addiction is the way it's eroding our ability to be present in the moment and truly connect with the people around us. How often have you been out with friends or family, only to find everyone staring at their phones instead of engaging with each other? It's a sad reality of our digital age, but one that can have serious consequences for our relationships and overall happiness.

So, what can we do about it? That's where digital detox comes in. By consciously unplugging from our devices for a period of time, we give ourselves the chance to recharge, both physically and mentally. It's like hitting the reset button on our brains, allowing us to step back from the constant barrage of information and stimuli and reconnect with ourselves and the world around us.

It is not easy, especially when we're so used to being constantly connected. That's why it's important to approach digital detox with a plan and realistic expectations.

Start by setting some ground rules for yourself. Decide how long you want to detox for—whether it's a few hours, a day, a weekend, or even longer—and stick to it. Let your friends and family know that you'll be taking a break from your devices so they don't worry when they don't hear from you.

Next, identify your digital triggers—the times and situations when you're most likely to reach for your phone out of habit—and come up with alternative activities to occupy your time. Maybe it's reading a book, going for a walk, or spending time with loved ones. Find what works for you and make a conscious effort to prioritize those activities over mindless screen time.

And finally, be gentle with yourself. Breaking habits takes time, and it's okay if you slip up occasionally. The important thing is to keep trying and to be mindful of how your digital habits are affecting your life.

In the end, digital detox is all about finding balance in our increasingly digital world. It's about taking back control of our time and attention, and reclaiming the moments that truly matter. So why not give it a try? You might just be surprised at how much better you feel when you unplug and reconnect with the world around you.

The Benefits of Digital Detox

In today's fast-paced world, we are constantly bombarded with digital distractions. However, taking a step back and disconnecting from our devices can have profound benefits for our mental, emotional, and physical well-being.

Improved Mental Clarity:

One of the most significant benefits of digital detox is the improvement in mental clarity. When we are constantly glued to our screens, our brains become overloaded with information, making it difficult to focus and concentrate. Taking a break from digital devices allows our minds to rest and recharge, leading to improved concentration, sharper memory, and enhanced cognitive function.

Reduced Stress and Anxiety:

Digital detox can also help reduce stress and anxiety levels. The constant barrage of notifications, emails, and social media updates can trigger feelings of overwhelm and anxiety. By disconnecting from our devices, we give ourselves permission to slow down and breathe, reducing cortisol levels and promoting a sense of calm and relaxation.

Better Sleep Quality:

Our digital devices emit blue light, which can disrupt our natural sleep-wake cycle and interfere with our ability to fall asleep and stay asleep. Digital detoxing before bedtime allows our bodies to wind down naturally, leading to better sleep quality and improved overall health. By disconnecting from screens, we can create a more conducive sleep environment and enjoy restorative sleep.

Enhanced Productivity:

Constant digital distractions can hinder our productivity and ability to focus on important tasks. Digital detoxing allows us to break free from the cycle of multitasking and constant interruptions, enabling us to devote our full attention to the task at hand. As a result, we can accomplish more in less time and experience a greater sense of satisfaction and accomplishment.

Stronger Relationships:

Spending excessive time on digital devices can take a toll on our relationships with others. Digital detoxing encourages us to be more present and engaged in our interactions with loved ones, fostering deeper connections and stronger bonds. By prioritizing face-to-face communication and quality time with family and friends, we can nurture meaningful relationships and create lasting memories.

Increased Creativity:

Disconnecting from digital devices allows our minds to wander and explore new ideas and perspectives. Without the constant barrage of information and stimuli, we are free to tap into our creativity and imagination, leading to new insights, innovative solutions, and fresh perspectives. Digital detoxing can reignite our passion for creative pursuits and inspire us to think outside the box.

Greater Self-Awareness:

Digital detoxing provides an opportunity for self-reflection and introspection. When we disconnect from the noise of the digital world, we can tune into our inner thoughts and feelings, gaining a deeper understanding of ourselves and our needs. By cultivating self-awareness, we can make more conscious choices and lead more fulfilling lives aligned with our values and priorities.

Improved Physical Health:

Excessive screen time is associated with a sedentary lifestyle, which can contribute to various health issues such as obesity, heart disease, and diabetes. Digital detoxing encourages us to get moving and engage in physical activities that promote overall health and well-being. Whether it's going for a walk in nature, practicing yoga, or playing sports, disconnecting from screens can help us lead a more active and healthy lifestyle.

Digital detoxing offers a multitude of benefits for our mental, emotional, and physical health. By taking a break from our digital devices, we can experience improved mental clarity, reduced stress and anxiety, better sleep quality, enhanced productivity, stronger relationships, increased creativity, greater self-awareness, and improved physical health. Incorporating regular digital detoxes into our lives can help us achieve a healthier balance between the digital world and the real world, leading to a more fulfilling and meaningful life.

Common Misconceptions About Digital Detox

In present day scenario, where digital devices are an integral part of daily life, the concept of digital detox has gained significant attention. However, amidst the buzz surrounding this topic, several misconceptions have emerged. We will show up some of the most common misconceptions about digital detox in simple language.

Digital Detox Means Completely Disconnecting from Technology:

One of the biggest misconceptions about digital detox is that it requires completely disconnecting from technology. While this may be the case for some individuals during specific detox periods, digital detox is more about finding a healthy balance in our relationship with technology. It's about being mindful of our digital habits and using technology in a way that enhances our well-being rather than detracts from it.

Digital Detox Is Only for People with Technology Addictions:

Another common misconception is that digital detox is only for people with severe technology addictions. While digital detox can certainly benefit individuals struggling with excessive screen time or smartphone addiction, it's also valuable for anyone looking to improve their overall well-being. Even those who don't consider themselves addicted to technology can benefit from taking periodic breaks and reassessing their digital habits.

Digital Detox Requires Going Off the Grid:

Many people believe that digital detox means going off the grid entirely—disconnecting from the internet, social media, and all digital devices. While this approach can be beneficial for some, it's not the only way to detox. Digital detox can be as simple as setting boundaries around screen time, reducing notifications, or designating tech-free zones in your home. The goal is to find a balance that works for you.

Digital Detox Is a One-Time Fix:

Some individuals mistakenly believe that digital detox is a one-time fix—a short-term solution to digital overload. However, true digital detox is an ongoing process—a lifestyle shift that requires continuous effort and mindfulness. It's about cultivating healthy digital habits and making intentional choices about how we engage with technology on a daily basis.

Digital Detox Means Missing Out on Important Information:

Another common concern about digital detox is the fear of missing out on important information, news, or social events. While it's true that taking a break from technology may result in temporarily missing out on certain updates, the benefits of digital detox—such as improved mental health, better sleep, and enhanced focus—far outweigh the potential drawbacks. Plus, there are plenty of ways to stay informed and connected offline, such as through face-to-face conversations, books, and community events.

Digital Detox Is Only About Disconnecting:

While disconnecting from technology is an important aspect of digital detox, it's not the only focus. True digital detox is about reconnecting—with ourselves, with our loved ones, and with the world around us. It's about rediscovering the simple pleasures of life that may have been overshadowed by digital distractions. By disconnecting from screens, we create space for meaningful connections and experiences that nourish our soul.

Digital Detox Is All or Nothing:

Some people believe that digital detox requires an all-or-nothing approach—either you're fully engaged with technology or completely disconnected. However, digital detox is not about extremes; it's about finding a middle ground that works for you. You don't have to give up technology altogether to reap the benefits of a digital detox. Instead, focus on moderation and mindfulness in your digital usage.

Digital Detox Is Easy:

Contrary to popular belief, digital detox is not always easy. In fact, it can be quite challenging, especially in today's hyper-connected world. Breaking free from ingrained habits and dependencies takes time and effort. It requires self-discipline, resilience, and a willingness to embrace discomfort. However, the rewards of digital detox—such as increased mindfulness, improved relationships, and enhanced well-being—are well worth the effort.

Finally, digital detox is a valuable practice that can help us reclaim control over our digital lives and reconnect with what truly matters. By discrediting these common misconceptions and embracing a more balanced approach to technology, we can develop a healthier relationship with technology and live more fulfilling lives offline and online.

Assessing Your Digital Dependency

While technology has undoubtedly revolutionized the way we live, work, and communicate, excessive use can lead to negative consequences. From decreased productivity and impaired concentration to strained relationships and mental health issues, the effects of digital dependency can be far-reaching.

- **Signs of Digital Overload**

    While technology has undoubtedly made our lives easier in many ways, it's essential to recognize when our digital consumption reaches unhealthy levels. Here are some signs that you may be experiencing digital overload:

    Constant Connectivity: Do you find yourself constantly checking your phone for notifications, even when you're supposed to be relaxing or spending time with loved ones? Constant connectivity can be a sign of digital overload, as it indicates a compulsive need to stay plugged in at all times.

Difficulty Disconnecting: Have you ever tried to take a break from technology, only to find yourself feeling anxious or restless? Difficulty disconnecting from digital devices, even for short periods, can indicate that you're overly reliant on technology for stimulation and entertainment.

Increased Screen Time: Pay attention to how much time you spend in front of screens each day. If you find yourself spending hours scrolling through social media, watching videos online, or playing games on your phone, it may be a sign that you're experiencing digital overload.

Physical Symptoms: Excessive screen time can also take a toll on your physical health. Headaches, eye strain, and neck pain are common symptoms of digital overload, as they can result from prolonged periods of staring at screens without taking breaks.

Neglecting Responsibilities: Are you neglecting important tasks and responsibilities in favor of spending time online? If you find yourself procrastinating on work or chores because you're too busy browsing the internet or chatting with friends online, it may be a sign that your digital habits are out of balance.

Impact on Sleep: The blue light emitted by screens can disrupt your sleep patterns and make it difficult to fall asleep at night. If you find yourself staying up late to browse the internet or check social media, it may be affecting your quality of sleep and leaving you feeling tired and irritable during the day.

Social Withdrawal: Digital overload can also lead to social withdrawal and isolation. If you find yourself spending more time interacting with people online than in person, it may be a sign that your digital habits are interfering with your real-life relationships.

Mental Health Issues: Excessive screen time has been linked to an increased risk of mental health issues such as anxiety, depression, and low self-esteem. If you notice changes in your mood or mental well-being after spending time online, it may be a sign that you need to take a step back and reevaluate your digital habits.

Inability to Focus: Digital overload can also affect your ability to concentrate and focus on tasks. If you find yourself constantly switching between tabs on your computer or checking your phone while trying to work or study, it may be a sign that your digital habits are hindering your productivity.

Feeling Overwhelmed: Lastly, feeling overwhelmed by the constant stream of information and stimuli online can be a sign of digital overload. If you find yourself feeling stressed, anxious, or mentally exhausted after spending time online, it may be a sign that you need to take a break and prioritize self-care.

By being mindful of your screen time, setting boundaries, and prioritizing self-care, you can avoid the negative consequences of digital overload and enjoy a more balanced and fulfilling life.

Assessing Personal Digital Habits

Taking stock of your personal digital habits is essential for understanding your level of dependency. Ask yourself the following questions:

- How much time do I spend on digital devices each day?

- What activities do I engage in online, and are they enhancing or detracting from my quality of life?
- Do I feel anxious or stressed when I'm unable to access digital devices or social media?
- How do my digital habits impact my relationships with friends, family, and colleagues?
- Am I able to disconnect from technology and enjoy offline activities without feeling restless or bored?

By honestly assessing your digital habits and their impact on your life, you can gain valuable insights into your level of dependency and identify areas for improvement.

Setting Clear Goals

Once you've assessed your digital dependency, it's time to set clear goals for reducing or managing your screen time. Start by identifying areas where you'd like to make changes, whether it's reducing social media usage, limiting screen time before bed, or setting boundaries around device use during family time.

Establishing Boundaries and Limits

Establishing boundaries and limits around your digital usage is key to breaking free from dependency. Consider implementing the following strategies:

- Designate technology-free zones in your home, such as the dining room or bedroom, where digital devices are off-limits.
- Set specific times during the day when you'll engage in digital activities, and stick to these boundaries to avoid mindless scrolling or excessive screen time.
- Use apps or built-in features on your devices to track your screen time and set daily limits for specific apps or categories.
- Preparing Yourself Mentally and Emotionally

Breaking free from digital dependency requires a mental and emotional shift. Prepare yourself for potential challenges and setbacks along the way, and be gentle with yourself as you navigate this process of change. Seek support from friends, family, or mental health professionals if needed, and celebrate your progress as you work towards a healthier relationship with technology.

Assessing your digital dependency is a crucial step towards finding balance and reclaiming control over your digital habits. By recognizing the signs of digital overload, understanding the impact on your mental and physical health, and taking proactive steps to set boundaries and limits, you can break free from dependency and cultivate a healthier relationship with technology. It is never too late to reassess your digital habits and make positive changes for a happier, more fulfilling life offline.

Assessing Personal Digital Habits

While technology offers many benefits, it's important to assess our personal digital habits to ensure they're not negatively impacting our well-being. In this article, we'll explore some simple ways to assess and reflect on our digital habits.

Start by Observing Your Usage Patterns The first step in assessing your digital habits is to observe how and when you use your devices. Take note of the amount of time you spend on your smartphone, computer, and other digital devices throughout the day. Pay attention to patterns such as checking your phone first thing in the morning or mindlessly scrolling through social media before bed. These observations can provide valuable insights into your digital habits and help you identify areas for improvement.

Reflect on Your Emotional Responses:

Next, reflect on how your digital usage makes you feel. Do you feel anxious or stressed when you're away from your phone? Do you find yourself comparing your life to others on social media? Pay attention to any negative emotions that arise during or after using digital devices. These emotions can be indicators of unhealthy digital habits and can help guide you towards more mindful usage.

Consider the Impact on Your Relationships:

Think about how your digital habits affect your relationships with others. Do you find yourself distracted by your phone when spending time with friends or family? Are you able to fully engage in conversations without constantly checking your device? Reflect on how your digital usage may be impacting your ability to connect with others and nurture meaningful relationships.

Evaluate Your Productivity Levels:

Assess how your digital habits impact your productivity and focus. Do you find yourself easily distracted by notifications and social media while working or studying? Are you able to stay focused on tasks without constantly switching between apps or websites? Consider how your digital usage may be affecting your ability to concentrate and accomplish your goals.

Take Note of Physical Symptoms:

Pay attention to any physical symptoms that may arise from excessive digital usage. Do you experience headaches, eye strain, or neck pain after spending long periods of time on your devices? These physical symptoms can be signs of digital fatigue and may indicate that you need to take breaks and limit your screen time.

Identify Triggers and Temptations:

Identify any triggers or temptations that lead to excessive digital usage. Do you reach for your phone out of boredom, loneliness, or habit? Are there specific apps or websites that you find particularly addictive? By identifying your triggers, you can develop strategies to resist temptation and cultivate healthier digital habits.

Assess Your Sleep Patterns:

Consider how your digital habits impact your sleep quality and quantity. Do you use your phone or tablet in bed before going to sleep? Do you find yourself staying up late to browse the internet or watch videos? Evaluate whether your digital usage is interfering with your ability to get a good night's sleep and consider implementing a digital curfew to improve your sleep hygiene.

Set Goals for Improvement:

Based on your observations and reflections, set realistic goals for improving your digital habits. This could include reducing your screen time, setting boundaries around when and where you use your devices, or implementing digital detox days where you unplug completely. Start small and gradually work towards your goals, celebrating your progress along the way.

Assessing your personal digital habits is an important step towards cultivating a healthier relationship with technology. By observing your usage patterns, reflecting on your emotional responses, and considering the impact on your relationships, productivity, and well-being, you can identify areas for improvement and make positive changes. By setting goals for improvement and implementing strategies to resist temptation, you can regain control of your digital habits and enjoy a more balanced and fulfilling life.

Planning Your Digital Detox

Planning your digital detox is essential for several reasons. Firstly, it allows you to set clear goals and objectives for your detox journey. Whether you're aiming to reduce screen time, break a social media addiction, or simply reconnect with the world around you, having a clear plan in place will help you stay focused and motivated.

Secondly, planning helps you establish boundaries and limits around your digital usage. By determining when and where you will use your devices, as well as setting guidelines for acceptable usage, you can create a structured environment that supports your detox goals. This might involve designating technology-free zones in your home, such as the dinner table or the bedroom, or setting specific time limits for device usage each day.

Additionally, planning your digital detox allows you to prepare yourself mentally and emotionally for the challenges ahead. Breaking free from digital dependence can be hard, and it's important to acknowledge and address any fears or concerns you may have about disconnecting. By taking the time to reflect on your motivations for detoxing and identifying potential obstacles, you can better equip yourself to navigate the ups and downs of the detox process.

Furthermore, planning helps you identify potential triggers and temptations that may derail your detox efforts. Whether it's the allure of a buzzing notification or the temptation to check your email "just one more time," knowing what might trip you up allows you to proactively address these challenges and find alternative coping strategies.

Finally, planning your digital detox gives you a roadmap to follow and a sense of accountability for your actions. By outlining the steps you will take to achieve your detox goals, you create a clear path forward that you can refer back to whenever you feel lost or overwhelmed. Moreover, sharing your plan with friends or family members can provide you with additional support and encouragement along the way.

Planning your digital detox is a crucial step towards reclaiming control over your digital habits and reconnecting with the world around you. By setting clear goals, establishing boundaries, preparing yourself mentally and emotionally, identifying triggers, and creating a roadmap for success, you can embark on your detox journey with confidence and determination. So take the time to plan your digital detox today and take the first step towards a healthier, more balanced relationship with technology.

Preparing Yourself Mentally and Emotionally

Whether we're facing challenges at work, navigating relationships, or simply trying to keep up with the demands of daily life, our mental and emotional resilience plays a crucial role in how we handle stress, setbacks, and uncertainty. Preparing yourself mentally and emotionally isn't just about putting on a brave face or suppressing your feelings—it's about building inner strength, resilience, and self-awareness to navigate life's ups and downs with grace and resilience. In this guide, we'll explore practical strategies and techniques to help you cultivate mental and emotional well-being, so you can face life's challenges with confidence and resilience.

Practice Self-Compassion:

One of the most important ways to prepare yourself mentally and emotionally is to practice self-compassion. Treat yourself with the same kindness and understanding that you would offer to a friend facing a difficult situation. Be gentle with yourself, especially during times of stress or self-doubt.

Cultivate Mindfulness:

Mindfulness is the practice of being present and fully engaged in the moment, without judgment or distraction. By cultivating mindfulness through practices such as meditation, deep breathing, or simply paying attention to your thoughts and feelings, you can develop greater self-awareness and resilience in the face of challenges.

Build Resilience:
Resilience is the ability to bounce back from setbacks and adversity with strength and determination. Building resilience involves developing coping skills, seeking support from others, and reframing negative thoughts into more positive and empowering ones. Remember that setbacks are a natural part of life, and they can be opportunities for growth and learning.

Prioritize Self-Care:
Taking care of your physical health is essential for maintaining mental and emotional well-being. Make sure to get enough sleep, eat a balanced diet, exercise regularly, and engage in activities that bring you joy and relaxation. Taking time for self-care isn't selfish—it's essential for replenishing your energy and resilience.

Practice Gratitude:
Cultivating an attitude of gratitude can have a powerful impact on your mental and emotional

well-being. Take time each day to reflect on the things you're grateful for, whether it's the support of loved ones, the beauty of nature, or the small moments of joy in your day. Gratitude can help shift your focus from what's lacking to what's abundant in your life.

Set Boundaries:

Setting healthy boundaries is essential for protecting your mental and emotional well-being. Learn to say no to commitments or activities that drain your energy or cause stress, and prioritize your own needs and priorities. Setting boundaries isn't about being selfish—it's about honoring your own limits and taking care of yourself.

Seek Support:

Don't be afraid to reach out for support when you need it. Whether it's talking to a trusted friend, family member, or therapist, seeking support from others can provide comfort, perspective, and validation during difficult times. Remember that asking for help is a sign of strength, not weakness.

Practice Relaxation Techniques:

Incorporate relaxation techniques such as deep breathing, progressive muscle relaxation, or guided imagery into your daily routine to help reduce stress and promote relaxation. These techniques can help calm your mind and body, and provide a sense of peace and tranquility in the midst of a busy day.

Cultivate Positive Relationships:

Building and nurturing positive relationships with friends, family, and community members can provide a sense of connection, belonging, and support during difficult times. Surround yourself with people who uplift and inspire you, and prioritize spending time with those who make you feel valued and appreciated.

Practice Emotional Regulation:

Learning to regulate your emotions is essential for maintaining mental and emotional well-being. Practice techniques such as deep breathing, journaling, or mindfulness to help you recognize and manage your emotions in healthy and constructive ways. Remember that emotions are a natural part of life, and it's okay to feel and express them.

Preparing yourself mentally and emotionally is an ongoing process that requires self-awareness, self-care, and self-compassion. By incorporating these strategies and techniques into your daily life, you can cultivate greater resilience, inner strength, and well-being, and face life's challenges with confidence and grace.

Strategies for Digital Detox

From smartphones and tablets to social media and streaming services, digital devices and platforms offer convenience, entertainment, and connectivity like never before. However, excessive screen time and constant connectivity can take a toll on our mental and physical well-being, leading to stress, anxiety, and burnout. That's where digital detox comes in—a deliberate effort to disconnect from technology and reclaim balance in our lives. Here's few simple strategies for digital detox that anyone can implement to find peace, clarity, and joy in an increasingly digital world.

The first step in digital detox is to establish clear boundaries around your technology use. Decide on specific times of the day when you will unplug from screens, such as during meals, before bedtime, or on weekends. Create designated technology-free zones in your home, such as the bedroom or dining area, where devices are not allowed.

Instead of spending hours scrolling through social media or binge-watching Netflix, prioritize offline activities that nourish your mind, body, and soul. Take up hobbies like gardening, painting, or cooking. Spend time outdoors hiking, biking, or simply enjoying nature. Connect with loved ones through face-to-face conversations, board games, or shared experiences.

Mindfulness is the practice of being present in the moment without judgment. Incorporate mindfulness techniques into your daily routine to help reduce stress and cultivate inner peace. Practice deep breathing exercises, meditation, or yoga to quiet the mind and center yourself. Pay attention to your thoughts, emotions, and sensations without getting swept away by digital distractions.

Set limits on your daily screen time to prevent mindless scrolling and excessive use of digital devices. Use apps or built-in features on your devices to track your screen time and set reminders when you've reached your limit.

Consider implementing a digital curfew, where you disconnect from screens an hour before bedtime to promote better sleep.

Replace digital activities with analog alternatives to reduce your dependence on technology. Instead of reading e-books, opt for traditional paper books or magazines. Write letters or journal entries by hand instead of sending emails or typing notes on your computer. Engage in analog hobbies like knitting, woodworking, or playing musical instruments.

Cultivate meaningful connections with friends, family, and community members in the real world. Schedule regular face-to-face interactions, whether it's grabbing coffee with a friend, attending a local event, or volunteering in your community. Invest time and energy in nurturing relationships that bring joy, support, and fulfillment to your life.

Declutter your digital space by organizing and minimizing your digital footprint. Delete unused apps, unsubscribe from unnecessary email lists, and unfollow accounts that no longer serve you. Streamline your digital environment to reduce distractions and create a more focused and productive workspace.

Prioritize self-care practices to nourish your mind, body, and spirit. Make time for activities that promote relaxation, such as taking a bubble bath, practicing aromatherapy, or indulging in a spa day. Get plenty of restorative sleep, eat a balanced diet, and exercise regularly to support your overall well-being.

Digital detox is not about perfection but progress. It's okay to slip up occasionally or feel tempted to check your phone or social media. Be gentle with yourself and practice self-compassion as you navigate the challenges of reducing your digital dependence. Celebrate small victories and acknowledge the effort you're putting into reclaiming balance in your life.

Finally, don't hesitate to seek support from friends, family, or mental health professionals if you're struggling to break free from digital addiction. Join online or offline support groups, attend workshops or seminars on digital wellness, and surround yourself with like-minded individuals who share your commitment to living a balanced and mindful life.

Digital detox is a journey of self-discovery and self-care—a conscious effort to reclaim control over our digital habits and find balance in an increasingly digital world. By implementing these simple strategies for digital detox, you can cultivate greater presence, joy, and fulfillment in your life, one mindful moment at a time.

Overcome Digital Challenges

In today's world of computers and smartphones, using technology can be tricky. It's easy to feel like we're missing out if we're not online all the time, and sometimes it's hard to take a break from social media. Dealing with these digital challenges can make us feel stressed and like we're not really connected to the world around us. But fear not, for with a little mindfulness and perseverance, we can overcome these challenges and reclaim control over our digital lives.

Dealing with FOMO (Fear of Missing Out):

FOMO, or the fear of missing out, is a common phenomenon in today's hyper-connected world. It's that nagging feeling we get when we see our friends posting pictures of exotic vacations, attending exciting events, or simply living their best lives while we're stuck at home scrolling through our feeds.

So how do we deal with FOMO and prevent it from consuming our lives?

Instead of focusing on what you're missing out on, try to appreciate the things you have in your life right now. Take a moment each day to reflect on the things you're grateful for, whether it's your family, your friends, or even just a warm cup of coffee in the morning.

While social media can be a great way to stay connected with friends and family, it can also exacerbate feelings of FOMO. Consider setting limits on your social media use and taking regular breaks from your devices to focus on the present moment.

Everyone's journey is different, and comparing yourself to others will only lead to feelings of inadequacy. Instead of constantly comparing yourself to others, focus on your own goals and aspirations, and take pride in your own accomplishments.

Instead of chasing after superficial experiences in an attempt to keep up with others, focus on building meaningful connections with the people who matter most to you. Spend quality time with friends and family, engage in activities that bring you joy, and prioritize genuine connections over virtual ones.

By practicing gratitude, limiting social media use, focusing on your own journey, and cultivating meaningful connections, you can overcome FOMO and embrace the present moment with open arms.

Managing Social Media Withdrawal:

From keeping up with friends and family to staying informed about the latest news and trends, social media offers a wealth of opportunities for connection and engagement. However, excessive use of social media can also lead to withdrawal symptoms when we try to cut back or take a break.

So how do we manage social media withdrawal and create a healthier relationship with our devices?

Establish clear boundaries around your social media use and stick to them. Consider setting limits on the amount of time you spend on social media each day and designating specific times of day when you'll allow yourself to check your accounts.

Instead of turning to social media whenever you're bored or restless, try to find alternative activities that bring you joy and fulfillment. Whether it's reading a book, going for a walk, or spending time with loved ones, finding healthy ways to occupy your time can help reduce the urge to check your social media accounts.

When you feel the urge to check your social media accounts, take a moment to pause and check in with yourself. Ask yourself why you're feeling the need to turn to social media and whether there might be other ways to address your underlying emotions.

If you're struggling to manage social media withdrawal on your own, don't be afraid to reach out for support. Talk to friends or family members about your struggles, or consider seeking professional help from a therapist or counselor who can offer guidance and support.

By following all above activities, you can manage social media withdrawal and create a healthier relationship with your devices.

Coping with Digital Temptations and Relapses:

In today's digital age, temptation lurks around every corner. Whether it's the attraction of social media, the temptation to binge-watch Netflix, or the irresistible urge to check our email one last time before bed, digital temptations can often lead us down a slippery slope towards relapse.
So how do we cope with digital temptations and prevent relapses?

Take some time to identify the specific situations or emotions that tend to trigger your digital temptations. Whether it's boredom, stress, or loneliness, understanding your triggers can help you develop healthier coping mechanisms.

Once you've identified your triggers, create a plan for how you'll respond when temptation strikes. Whether it's going for a walk, practicing deep breathing exercises, or calling a friend for support, having a plan in place can help you resist the urge to give in to temptation.

If you do find yourself giving in to temptation and relapsing, don't be too hard on yourself. Remember that relapses are a normal part of the recovery process, and beating yourself up will only make it harder to get back on track. Instead, practice self-compassion and remind yourself that tomorrow is a new day.

Take some time to reflect on what led to your relapse and what you can do differently next time. Did you underestimate your triggers? Did you fail to stick to your plan? By learning from your mistakes, you can develop strategies to prevent future relapses and build resilience in the face of temptation.

By applying all these, you can cope with digital temptations and prevent relapses, ultimately leading to a healthier and more balanced relationship with technology.

Maintaining Digital Balance

In today's fast-paced digital age, finding balance between our online and offline lives can be challenging. With the constant bombardment of emails, social media notifications, and digital distractions, it's easy to feel overwhelmed and disconnected from the real world. However, by cultivating sustainable digital habits, building a supportive environment, and prioritizing real connections and experiences, we can reclaim control over our digital lives and find harmony in the modern world.

Creating Sustainable Digital Habits

The first step to maintaining digital balance is to establish sustainable habits that promote healthy use of technology. This means setting boundaries around our digital consumption, being mindful of our screen time, and prioritizing activities that nourish our minds, bodies, and souls.

One way to create sustainable digital habits is to set limits on our screen time. This might involve scheduling designated "digital detox" periods where we disconnect from our devices and engage in offline activities such as reading, exercising, or spending time with loved ones. By consciously allocating time for both digital and non-digital activities, we can strike a balance that allows us to enjoy the benefits of technology without becoming overwhelmed by its demands.

Another important aspect of creating sustainable digital habits is to be mindful of our online behaviors. This means being intentional about the content we consume, the interactions we engage in, and the impact of our digital footprint on ourselves and others. By practicing mindfulness and self-awareness, we can cultivate a healthier relationship with technology and reduce the negative effects of digital overload.

Building a Supportive Environment

In addition to cultivating personal habits, maintaining digital balance also requires creating a supportive environment that encourages healthy technology use. This involves setting boundaries with family, friends, and colleagues, as well as establishing norms and expectations around digital etiquette and communication.

One way to build a supportive digital environment is to communicate openly and honestly with those around us about our digital boundaries and preferences. This might involve setting guidelines for when and how we use technology in social settings, as well as being respectful of others' preferences and boundaries.

Another important aspect of building a supportive digital environment is to create designated "tech-free zones" in our homes and workplaces. These areas provide a sanctuary from digital distractions and allow us to focus on real-world interactions and experiences without the constant interruption of screens and notifications.

Learning to Prioritize Real Connections and Experiences

Ultimately, maintaining digital balance is about prioritizing real connections and experiences over digital distractions and superficial interactions. This means investing time and energy in nurturing meaningful relationships, engaging in activities that bring us joy and fulfillment, and being present in the moment.

One way to prioritize real connections and experiences is to practice active listening and empathy in our interactions with others. This involves putting aside our devices and distractions, truly engaging with those around us, and seeking to understand their thoughts, feelings, and perspectives. By fostering genuine connections with others, we can cultivate deeper relationships and a greater sense of belonging and connection in our lives.

Another important aspect of prioritizing real connections and experiences is to engage in activities that bring us joy and fulfillment outside of the digital realm. This might involve pursuing hobbies and interests that allow us to express ourselves creatively, explore new passions, and connect with others who share our interests. Whether it's spending time in nature, participating in community events, or simply enjoying quality time with loved ones, prioritizing real-world experiences enriches our lives and enhances our overall well-being.

Maintaining digital balance in an increasingly connected world requires intentionality, mindfulness, and a commitment to prioritizing what truly matters. By creating sustainable digital habits, building a supportive environment, and prioritizing real connections and experiences, we can reclaim control over our digital lives and find greater harmony, happiness, and fulfillment in the modern world

Book Summary

As we have learned from the book, finding balance is key to living a fulfilling and meaningful life. Embracing a balanced digital lifestyle means recognizing the value of technology while also prioritizing our well-being and relationships.

To achieve this balance, we must first become aware of our digital habits and how they impact our lives. Setting boundaries and limits around our screen time can help prevent technology from overshadowing the moments that truly matter. Whether it's designating tech-free zones in our homes or scheduling regular digital detoxes, small changes can make a big difference in restoring harmony to our lives.

It's also important to cultivate mindfulness and presence in our interactions with technology. Instead of mindlessly scrolling through social media feeds or constantly checking our devices, we can practice being fully present in the moment. This means savoring the sights, sounds, and sensations of the world around us, free from the distractions of screens.

By embracing a balanced digital lifestyle, we can reclaim control over our time and attention, allowing us to focus on the things that bring us joy and fulfillment. Whether it's spending quality time with loved ones, pursuing our passions, or simply enjoying the beauty of nature, there's a whole world waiting to be explored beyond the confines of our screens.

As we bring our journey to a close, I want to leave you with a few final words of encouragement and inspiration. Remember that you are not alone on this path towards digital wellness. There are countless others who share your struggles and are rooting for your success.

Be patient and compassionate with yourself as you navigate the ups and downs of this journey. Change takes time, and it's okay to take small steps forward, even if progress feels slow at times. Celebrate your successes, no matter how small, and use setbacks as opportunities for growth and learning.

Above all, your well-being is worth prioritizing. Your time and attention are precious commodities, and it's up to you to decide how you want to spend them. By embracing a balanced digital lifestyle, prioritizing self-care, and cultivating meaningful connections, you can create a life that is rich in fulfillment, joy, and purpose.

In this digital journey, I encourage you to stay true to yourself, stay connected to what matters most, and stay committed to your path towards digital wellness. You have the power to shape your own destiny, and I have every confidence that you will find success in this endeavor.

*Please scan for the other books of the **"Life Mastery"** Series.*

Other References

1) Free Courses
2) Join my Community
3) Want to be the Online Coach?